Get to grips with Handwriting with CGP!

Handwriting is an important skill to start learning in Reception — it takes practice, practice and more practice to get those letter shapes correct.

Luckily, that's exactly what this CGP book is for! It's packed full of handwriting activities, with an exercise for every day of autumn term.

And that's not all — every week there are fun activities to practise that all-important pencil control. It's perfect for getting pupils confident with handwriting, either in class or at home!

What CGP is all about

Our sole aim here at CGP is to produce the highest quality books — carefully written, immaculately presented and dangerously close to being funny.

Then we work our socks off to get them out to you — at the cheapest possible prices.

Contents

☑ Use the tick boxes to help keep a record of which pages have been attempted.

Week 1
- ☑ Day 1 1
- ☑ Day 2 2
- ☑ Day 3 3
- ☑ Day 4 4
- ☑ Day 5 5

Week 2
- ☑ Day 1 6
- ☑ Day 2 7
- ☑ Day 3 8
- ☑ Day 4 9
- ☑ Day 5 10

Week 3
- ☑ Day 1 11
- ☑ Day 2 12
- ☑ Day 3 13
- ☑ Day 4 14
- ☑ Day 5 15

Week 4
- ☑ Day 1 16
- ☑ Day 2 17
- ☑ Day 3 18
- ☑ Day 4 19
- ☑ Day 5 20

Week 5
- ☑ Day 1 21
- ☑ Day 2 22
- ☑ Day 3 23
- ☑ Day 4 24
- ☑ Day 5 25

Week 6
- ☑ Day 1 26
- ☑ Day 2 27
- ☑ Day 3 28
- ☑ Day 4 29
- ☑ Day 5 30

Week 7
- ☑ Day 1 31
- ☑ Day 2 32
- ☑ Day 3 33
- ☑ Day 4 34
- ☑ Day 5 35

Week 8
- ☑ Day 1 36
- ☑ Day 2 37
- ☑ Day 3 38
- ☑ Day 4 39
- ☑ Day 5 40

Week 9

- ☑ Day 1 41
- ☑ Day 2 42
- ☑ Day 3 43
- ☑ Day 4 44
- ☑ Day 5 45

Week 10

- ☑ Day 1 46
- ☑ Day 2 47
- ☑ Day 3 48
- ☑ Day 4 49
- ☑ Day 5 50

Week 11

- ☑ Day 1 51
- ☑ Day 2 52
- ☑ Day 3 53
- ☑ Day 4 54
- ☑ Day 5 55

Week 12

- ☑ Day 1 56
- ☑ Day 2 57
- ☑ Day 3 58
- ☑ Day 4 59
- ☑ Day 5 60

Published by CGP

ISBN: 978 1 78908 825 0

Editors: Sarah Pattison, Tamara Sinivassen and Hayley Thompson.
Reviewer: Juliette Green

With thanks to Gareth Mitchell and Glenn Rogers for the proofreading.
With thanks to Emily Smith for the copyright research.

Cover image and graphics used throughout the book © www.edu-clips.com.

Printed by Elanders Ltd, Newcastle upon Tyne.
Based on the classic CGP style created by Richard Parsons.

Text, design, layout and original illustrations © Coordination Group Publications Ltd. (CGP) 2021
All rights reserved.

Photocopying this book is not permitted, even if you have a CLA licence.
Extra copies are available from CGP with next day delivery • 0800 1712 712 • www.cgpbooks.co.uk

How to Use this Book

- This book contains 60 pages of daily handwriting practice.
- It's split into 12 sections — that's roughly one section for each week of the Reception Autumn term.
- A week is made up of 5 pages, so there's one for every school day of the term (Monday – Friday).
- Each page should take about 10 minutes to complete.
- The term starts off with pattern tracing to build pencil control and fine motor skills and leads on to letter formation. Numbers are also covered in this book.
- Day 5 of each week encourages pupils to practise their pencil control. It involves fun activities such as tracing pictures, along with Stripes the tiger. Colouring-in tasks are also spread throughout the book for extra practice.
- A typical page looks like this:

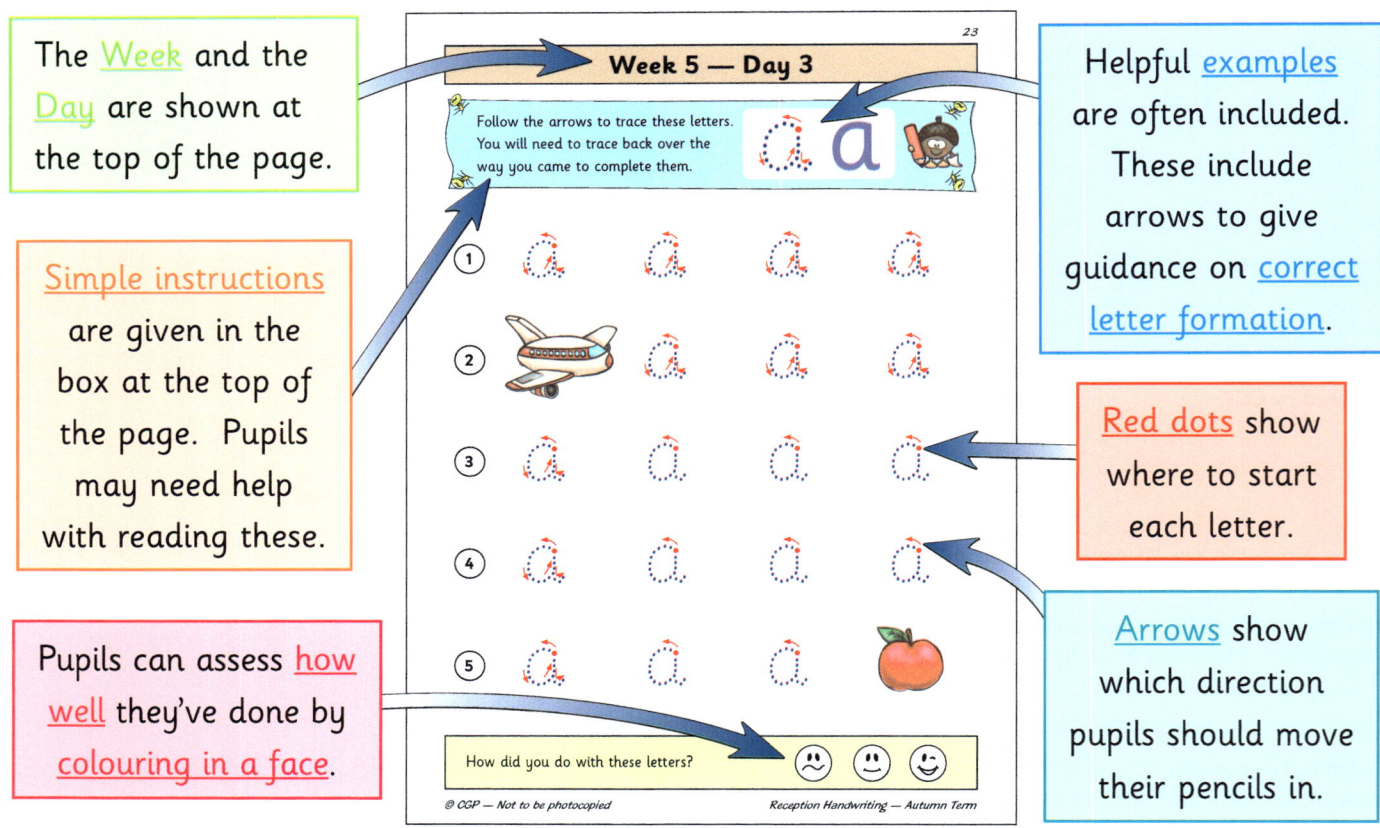

The Week and the Day are shown at the top of the page.

Simple instructions are given in the box at the top of the page. Pupils may need help with reading these.

Pupils can assess how well they've done by colouring in a face.

Helpful examples are often included. These include arrows to give guidance on correct letter formation.

Red dots show where to start each letter.

Arrows show which direction pupils should move their pencils in.

If you are a parent or guardian using this book at home with your child, you should bear in mind that different schools have different handwriting styles (e.g. '4' instead of '4'). You should check with the school to see how each letter is written. In this book, some of the letters have flicks at the bottom in preparation for joined-up writing.

Week 1 — Day 1

Start with your pencil on the red dots
and trace over these straight lines.
Try to keep your pencil on the page for each one.
When you've finished, colour in the flowers.

1.

2.

3.

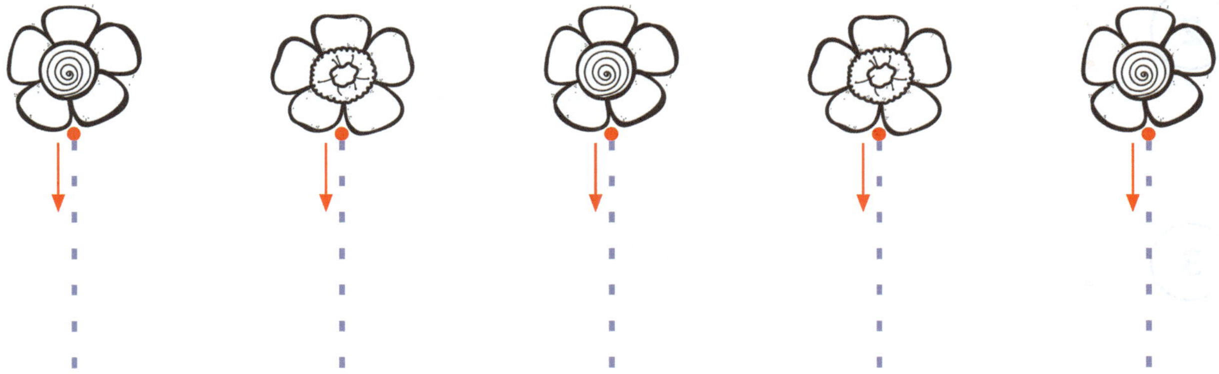

4.

How did you get on with these lines?

Week 1 — Day 2

Trace over these wavy lines.
Start with your pencil on the red dots.
Try to keep your pencil on the page for each line.
When you've finished, colour in the jellyfish.

1.

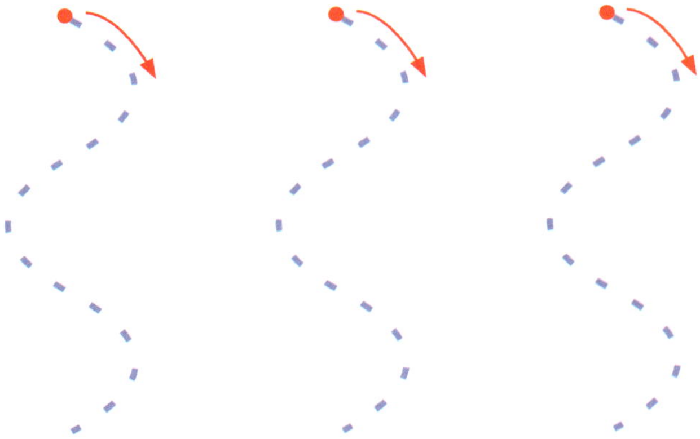

2.

3.

4.

How did you find tracing these lines?

Reception Handwriting — Autumn Term

Week 1 — Day 3

Start at the red dots and trace over these lines.
Try to keep your pencil on the page for each one.
Then colour in the balloons.

1.

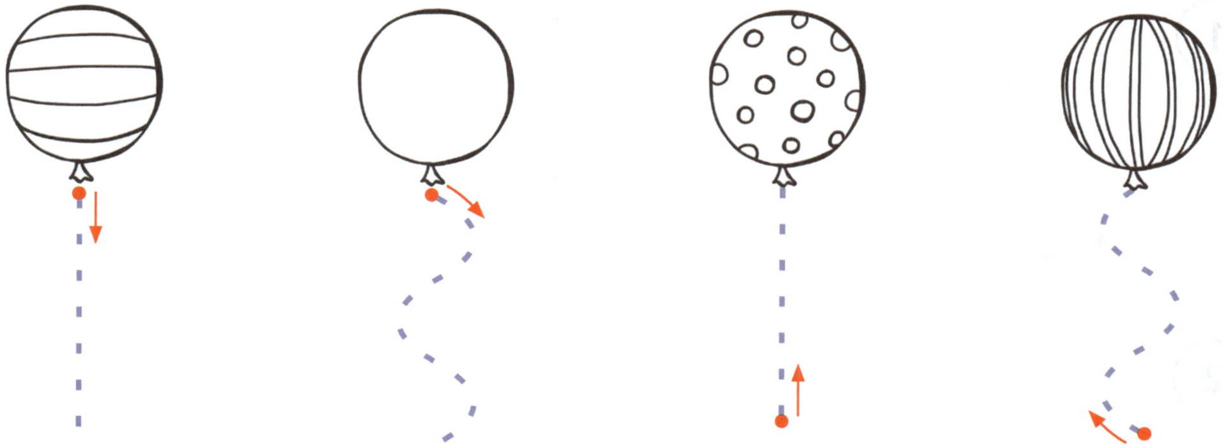

2.

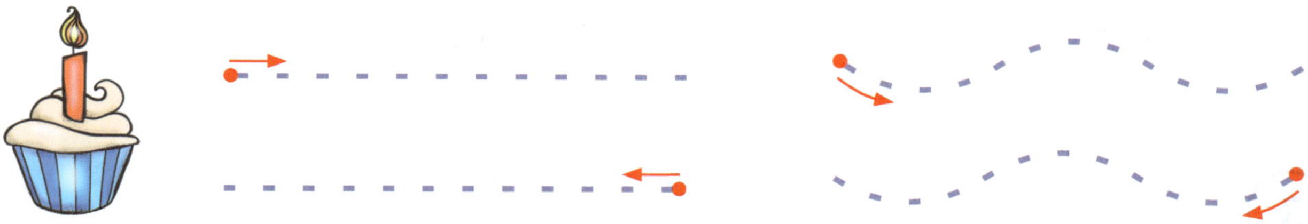

3.

4.

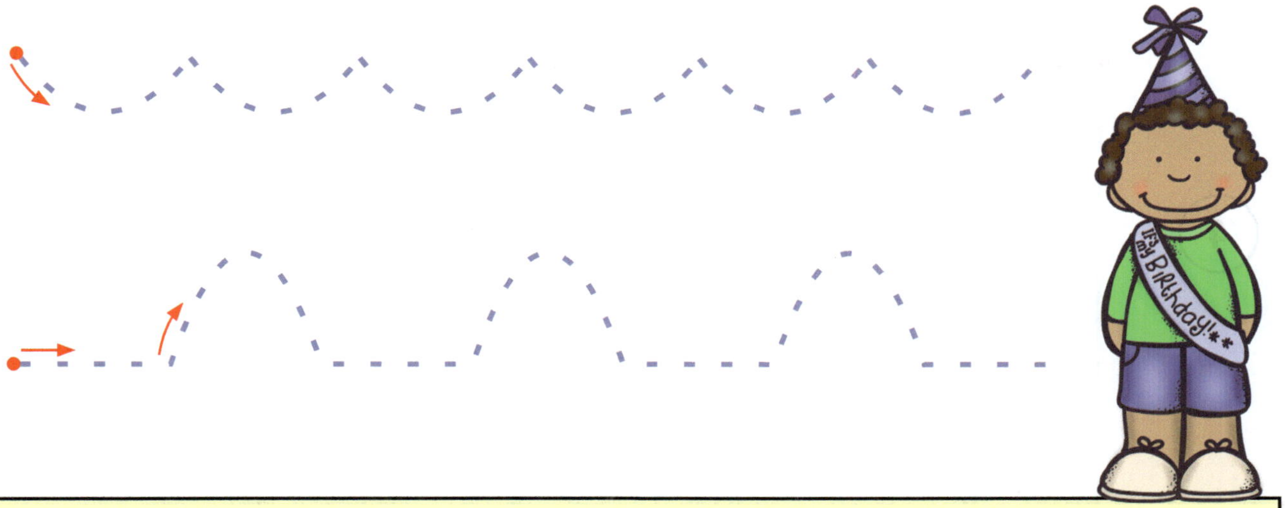

Did you trace all of these lines neatly?

Week 1 — Day 4

Trace the loops. Then colour in the butterflies. Remember to start with your pencil on the red dots.

1.

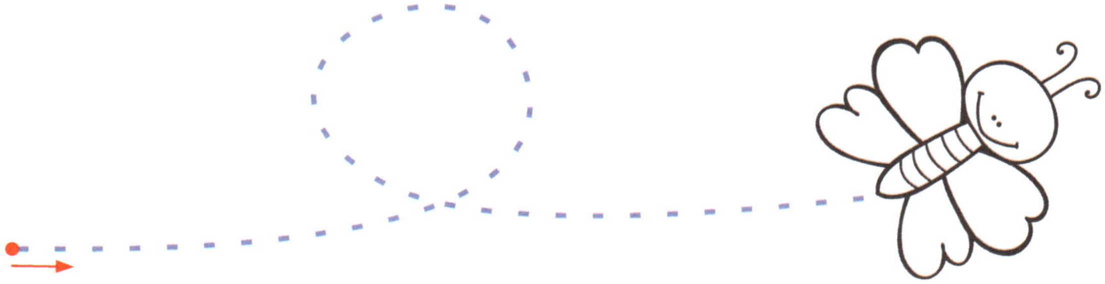

2.

3.

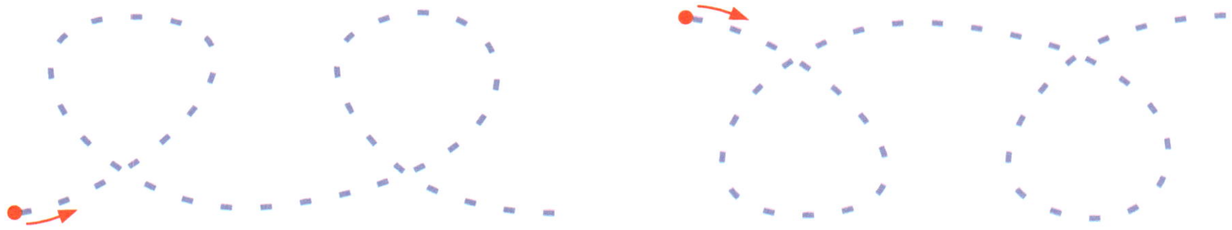

4.

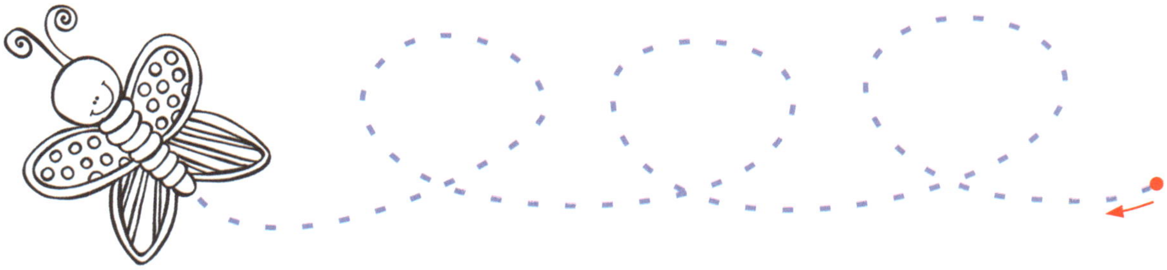

How well do you think you did today?

Week 1 — Day 5

Stripes has found a pirate treasure map.
Trace over the dashed line to show the path from the ship to the treasure. Then colour in the pirates and the treasure.

How did you get on with this map?

Week 2 — Day 2

Trace over these lines.
Start with your pencil on the red dots.
Try to keep your pencil on the page for each line.

How did you get on with these lines?

Week 2 — Day 3

Trace over these zigzags. Start with your pencil on the red dots. Then colour in the stars.

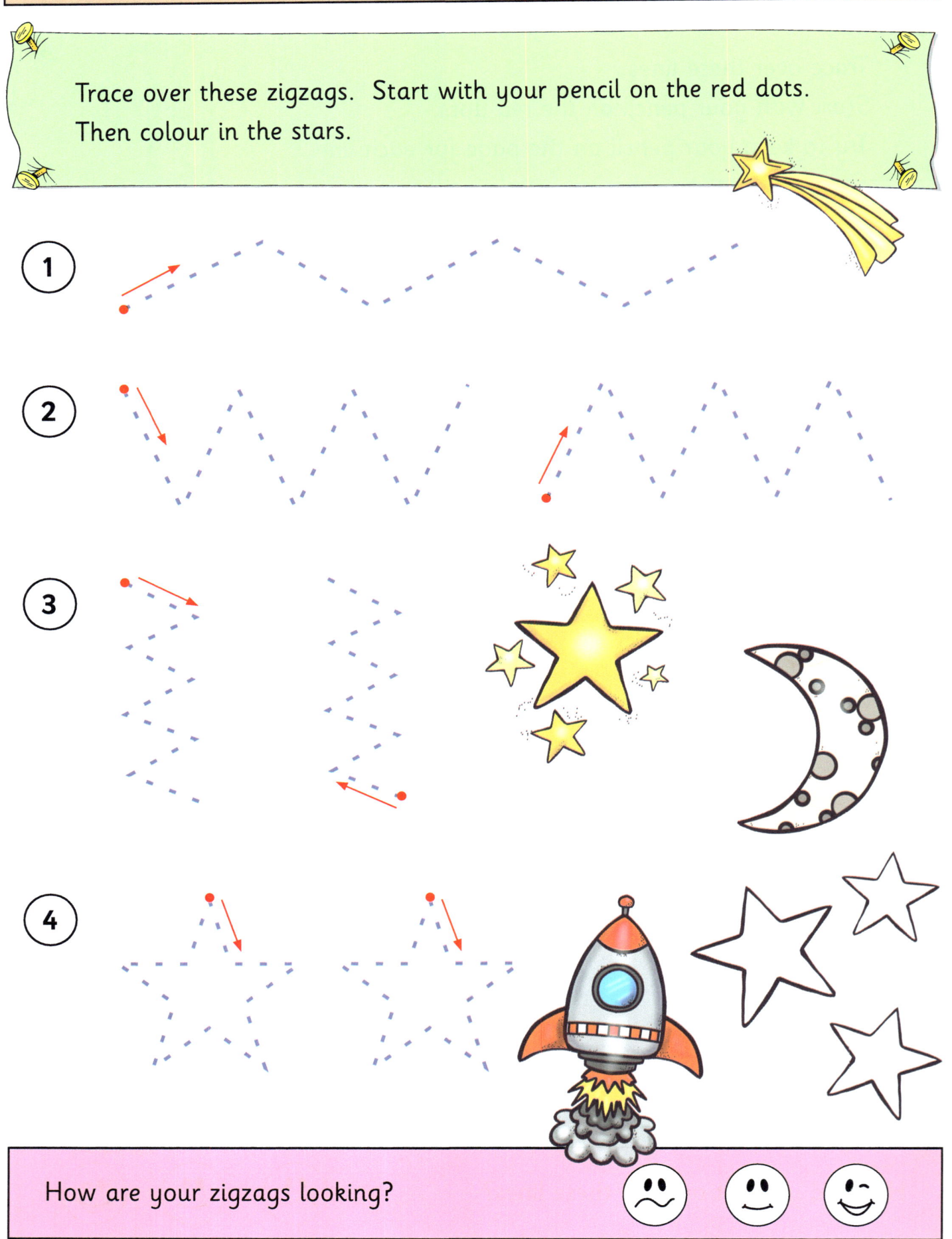

How are your zigzags looking?

Week 2 — Day 4

Trace over these lines.
Start with your pencil on the red dots.
Then colour in the cow.

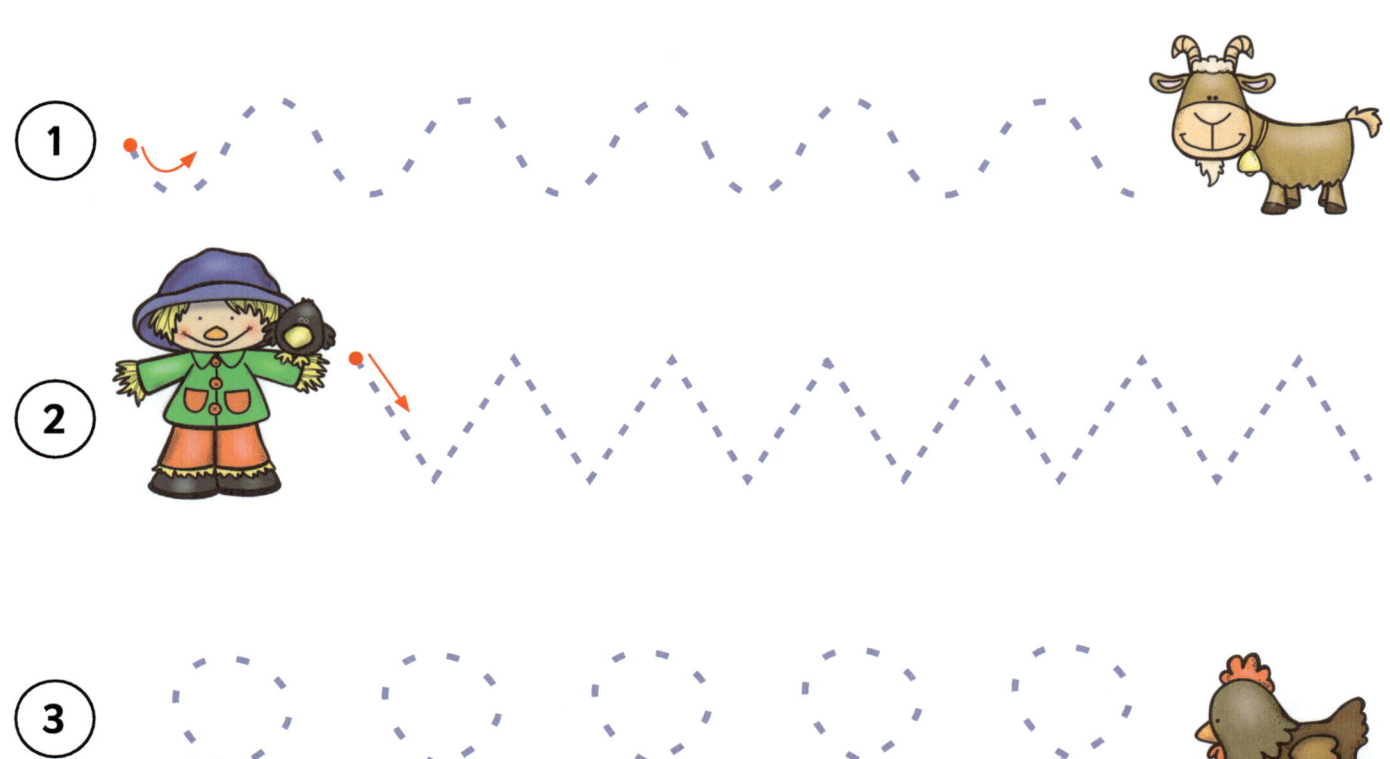

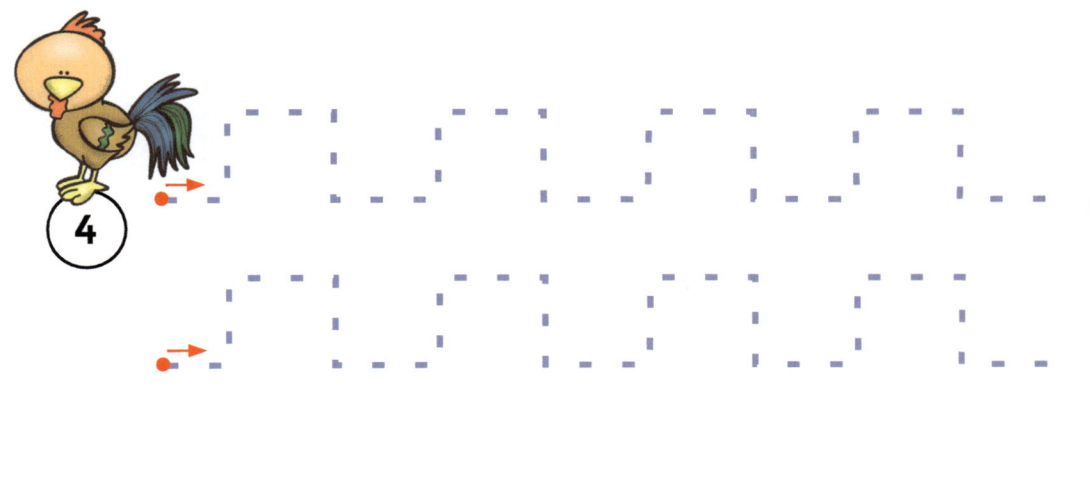

How did you get on today?

Week 2 — Day 5

Stripes has gone on a camping trip with some friends.
Draw over the blue lines to finish the picture of their trip.

How pleased are you with your picture?

Week 3 — Day 1

Start at the red dots and trace over these patterns.
Try to keep your pencil on the page as you trace each line.
Then give the caterpillar a face and legs, and colour it in.

1.

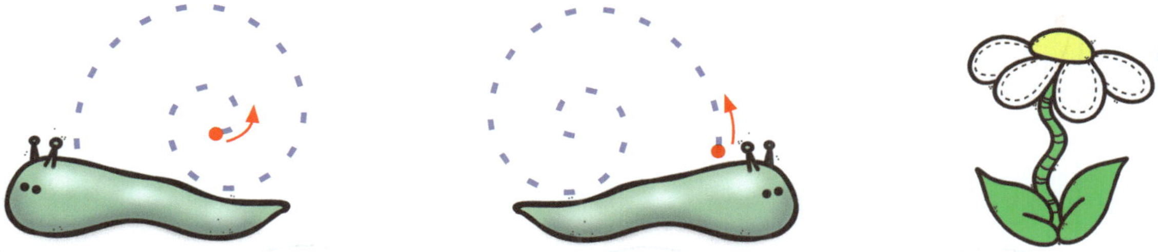

2.

3.

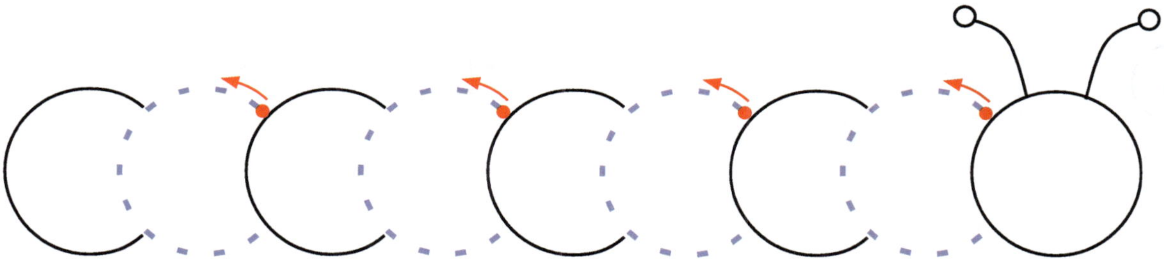

4.

5.

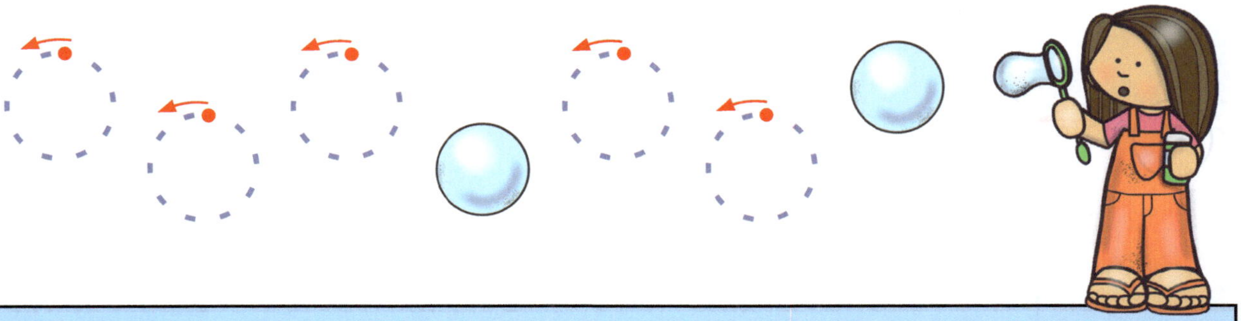

How did you get on with these patterns?

Week 3 — Day 2

Follow the arrows to trace these patterns.
Remember to start with your pencil on the red dot.
When you've finished, colour in the umbrellas.

1.

2.

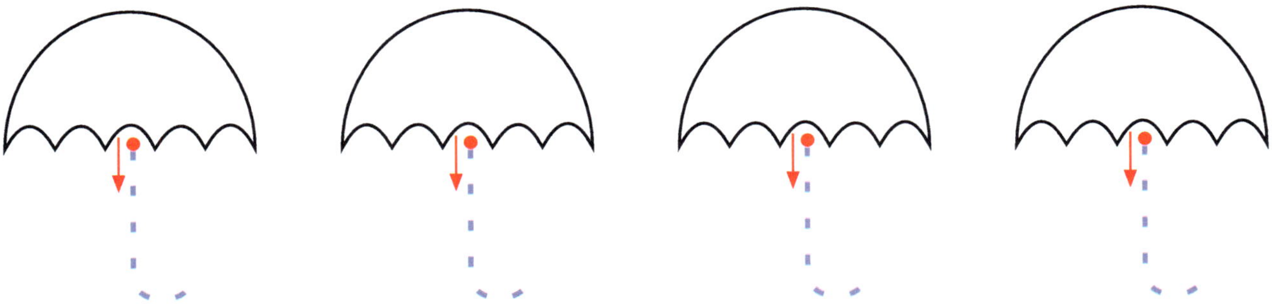

3.

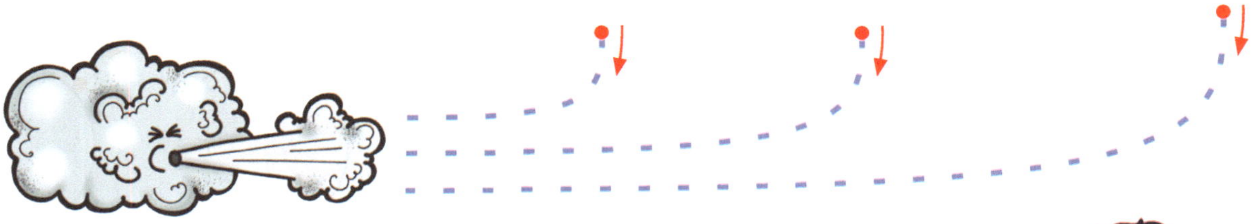

4.

5.

How well did you do with these patterns?

Week 3 — Day 3

Trace over these patterns. Start at the red dots and follow the arrows. For these patterns you have to move your pencil back over the way you came.

1.

2.

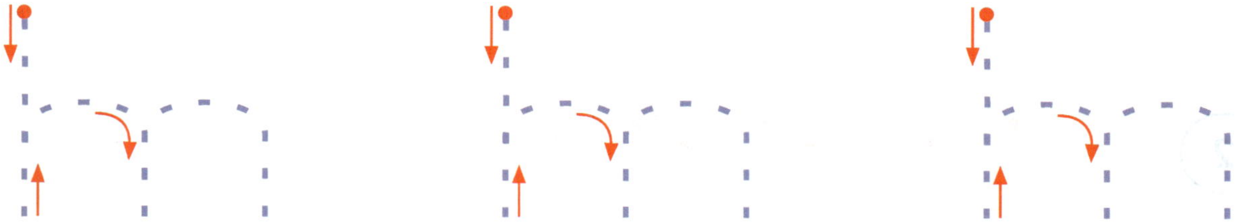

3.

4.

5.

How did you get on with this page?

Week 3 — Day 4

Trace over these patterns.
Start at the red dots and use the arrows to help you.
For the final pattern, you need to take your pencil off the page to draw each line.

1.

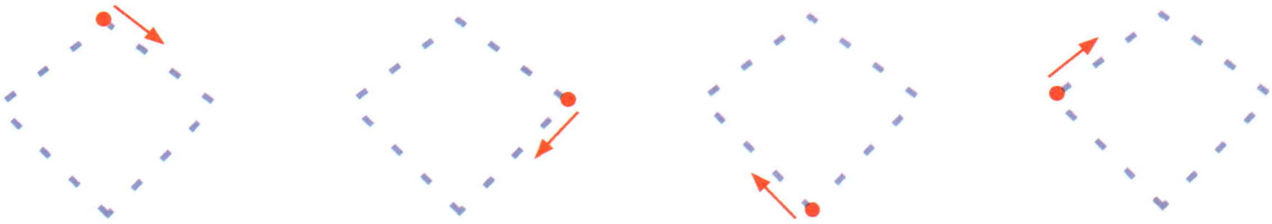

2.

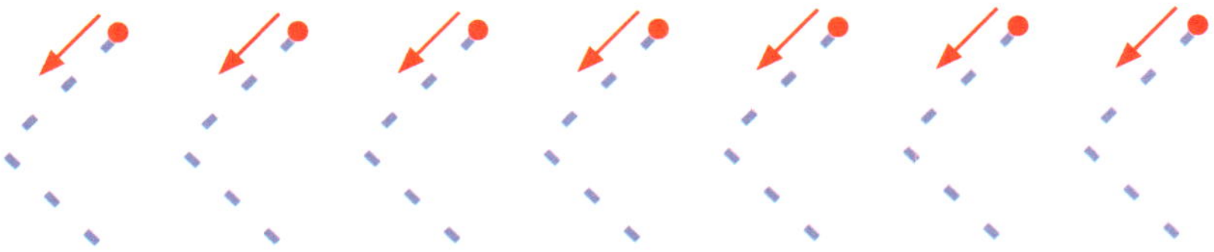

3.

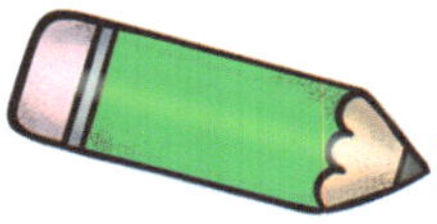

4.

5.

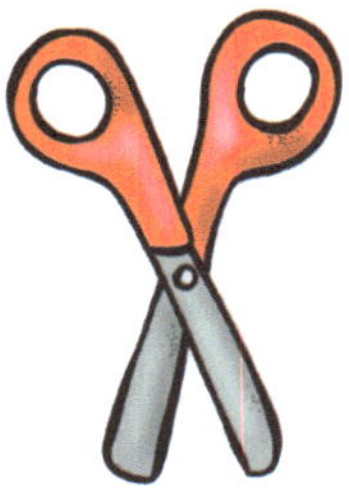

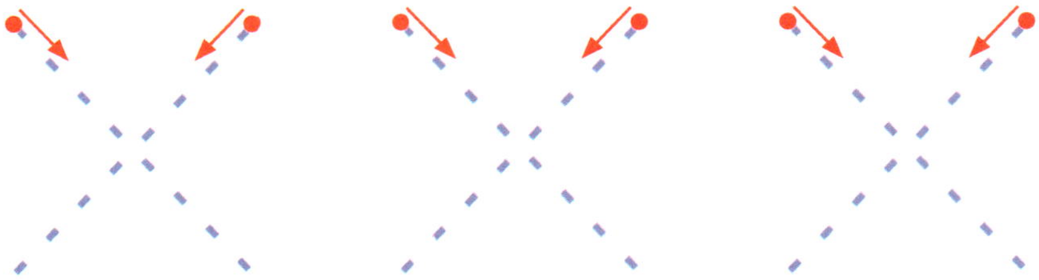

How did you find these patterns?

Reception Handwriting — Autumn Term

Week 3 — Day 5

Stripes is visiting the queen at her castle.
Draw over the blue lines to finish the picture.
Then colour in the queen.

How did you get on with this picture?

Week 4 — Day 1

Start at the red dots and trace over these patterns. Use the arrows to help you. Try to keep your pencil on the page as you trace each line. Then colour in the dog.

1.

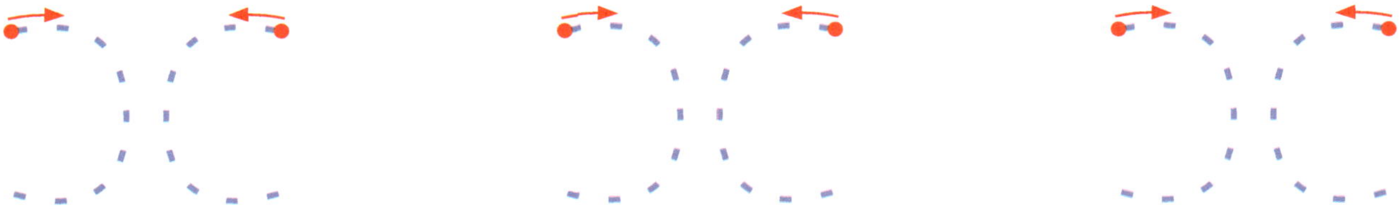

2.

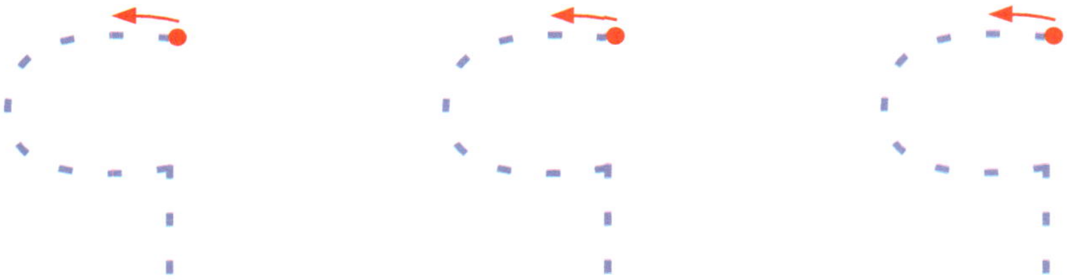

3.

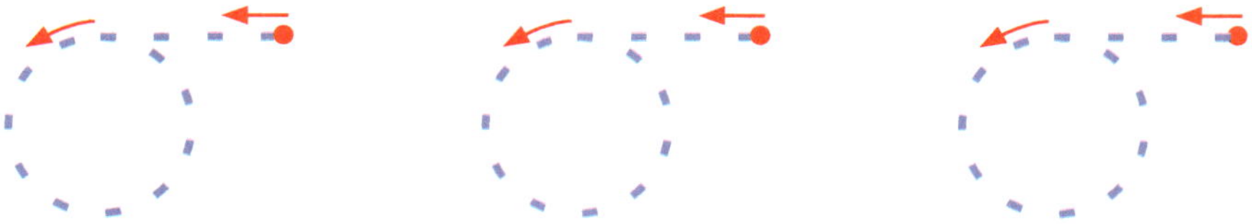

4.

5.

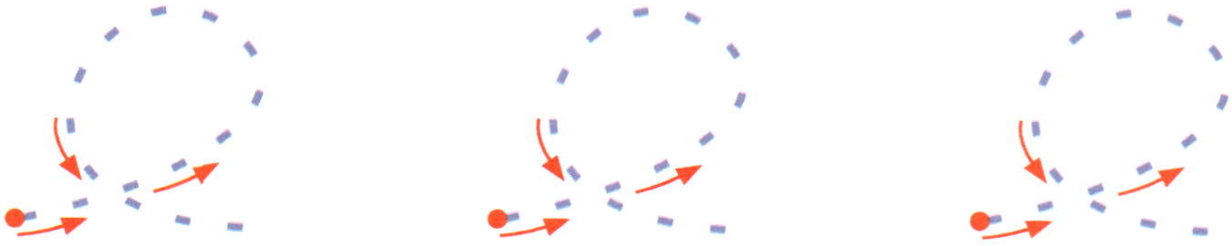

How did you find these patterns?

Reception Handwriting — Autumn Term

Week 4 — Day 2

Follow the arrows to trace over these patterns.
Remember to start with your pencil on the red dots.
When you've finished, colour in the rock star.

1.

2.

3.

4.

5.

How did you get on with these patterns?

Week 4 — Day 3

Trace over these patterns.
Start at the red dots and use the arrows to help you.
For these patterns, you have to trace back over the way you came.

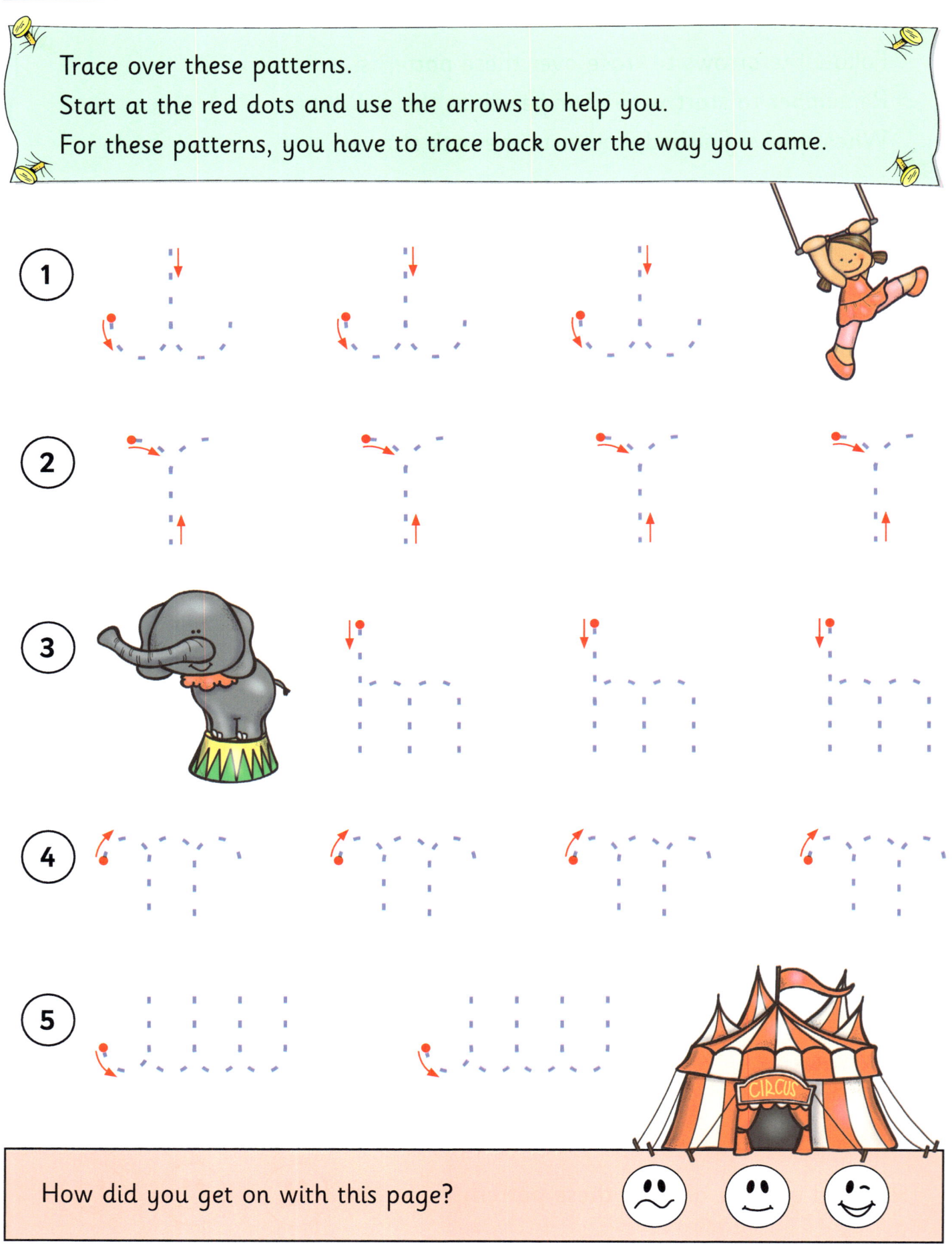

How did you get on with this page?

Week 4 — Day 4

Trace over these patterns.
Start at the red dots and follow the arrows.
When you've finished, colour in the cowboy.

1.

2.

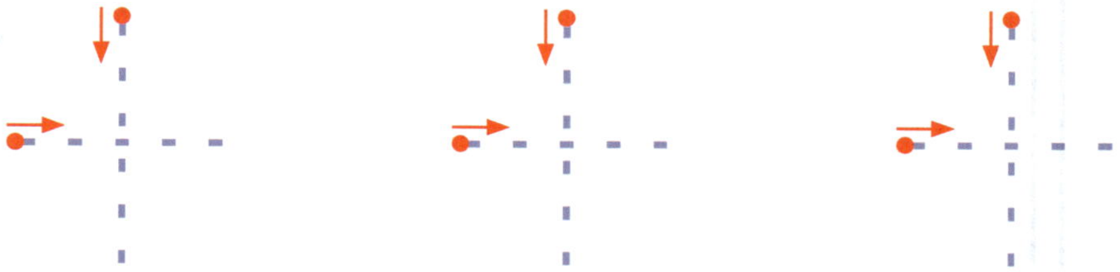

3.

4.

5.

How well did you trace these patterns?

Week 4 — Day 5

Stripes is drawing a picture of a dinosaur.
Trace over the dashed lines to finish the picture.
Then colour it in.

How did you get on with this picture?

Week 5 — Day 1

Start at the red dots and follow the arrows to trace these letters. When you've finished, colour in the camel.

1. c c c c
2. c c c c
3. c c c c 
4. c c c
5. c c c c

How did you get on with these letters?

Week 5 — Day 2

Follow the arrows to trace these letters.
Start at the red dot each time.
When you've finished, colour in the octopus.

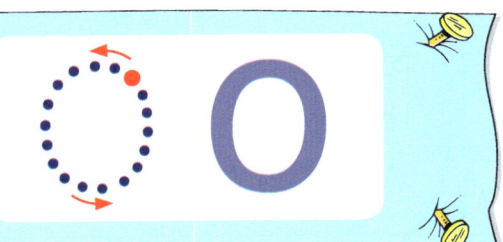

1

2

3

4

5

How did you get on with this page?

Reception Handwriting — Autumn Term

Week 5 — Day 3

Follow the arrows to trace these letters. You will need to trace back over the way you came to complete them.

1)

2)

3)

4)

5)

How did you do with these letters?

Week 5 — Day 4

Start at the red dots and follow the arrows to trace these letters.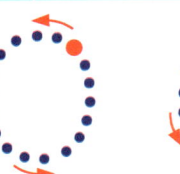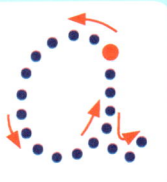

1

2

3

4

5

How well did you trace these letters?

Reception Handwriting — Autumn Term

Week 5 — Day 5

Stripes is watching the fireworks with some friends.
Trace over the blue lines to finish the picture.
Then colour in the squirrel and the fireworks.

How did you get on with this picture?

Week 6 — Day 1

Follow the arrows to trace these letters.
Start with your pencil on the red dot.
Don't forget to add the dot at the top.

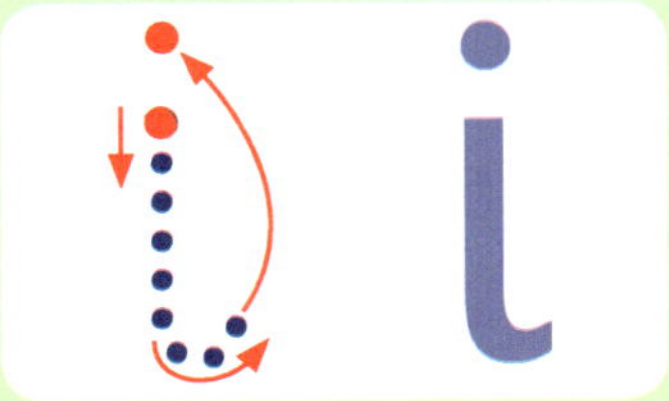

1.

2.

3.

4.

5.

How did you find tracing these letters?

Week 6 — Day 3

Follow the arrows to trace these letters. You will have to take your pencil off the page to cross the 't'.
When you've finished, colour in the turtle.

1.

2.

3.

4.

5.

How did you find this page?

Reception Handwriting — Autumn Term

Week 6 — Day 4

Trace these letters.
Use the arrows to help you.
Then colour in the ladybird.

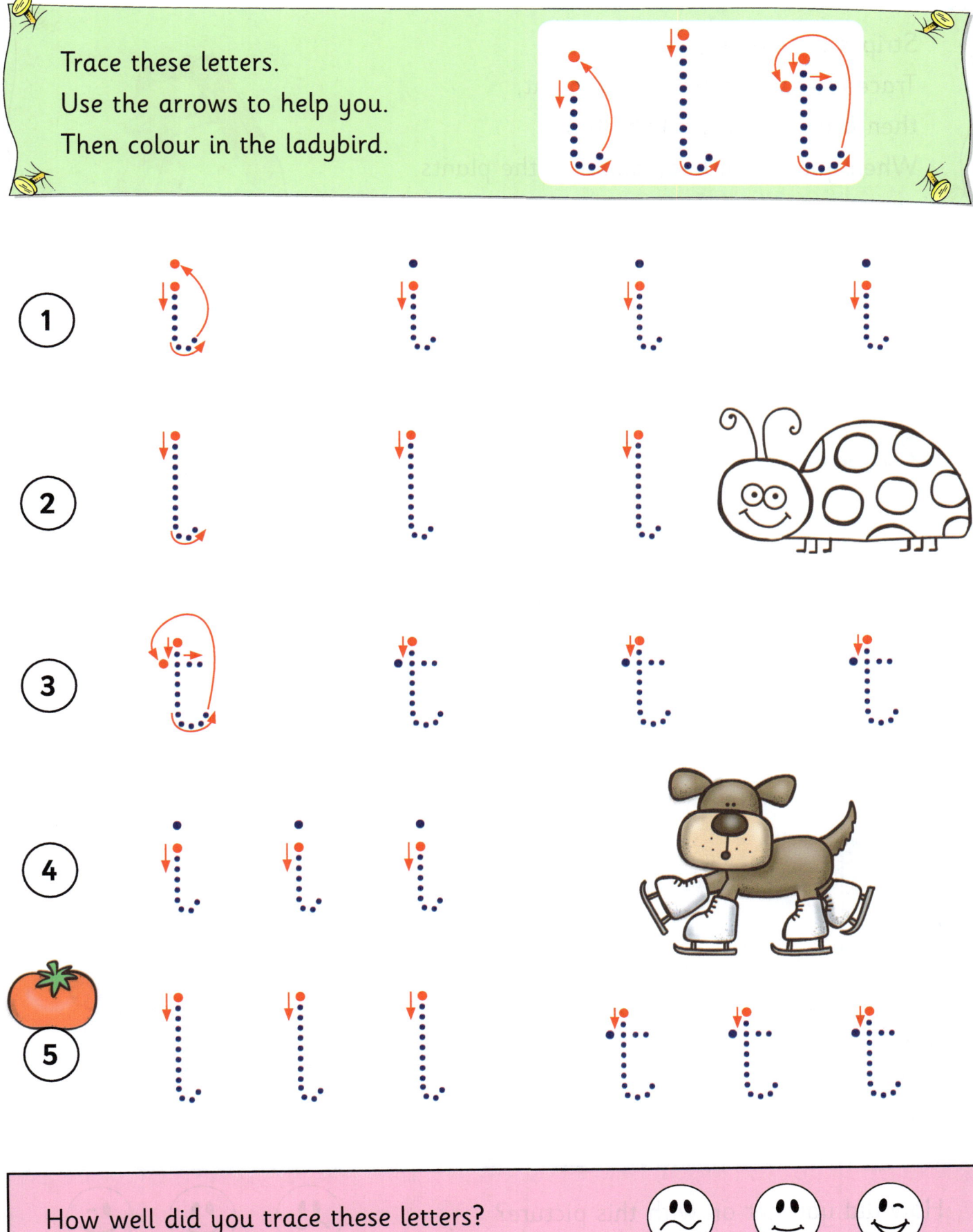

How well did you trace these letters?

Week 6 — Day 5

Stripes is watering the garden.
Trace over the leaves of the plant,
then draw a flower at the top.
When you've finished, colour in the plants.

How did you get on with this picture?

Week 7 — Day 1

Trace over the lines to complete the numbers. Start at the red dot each time.

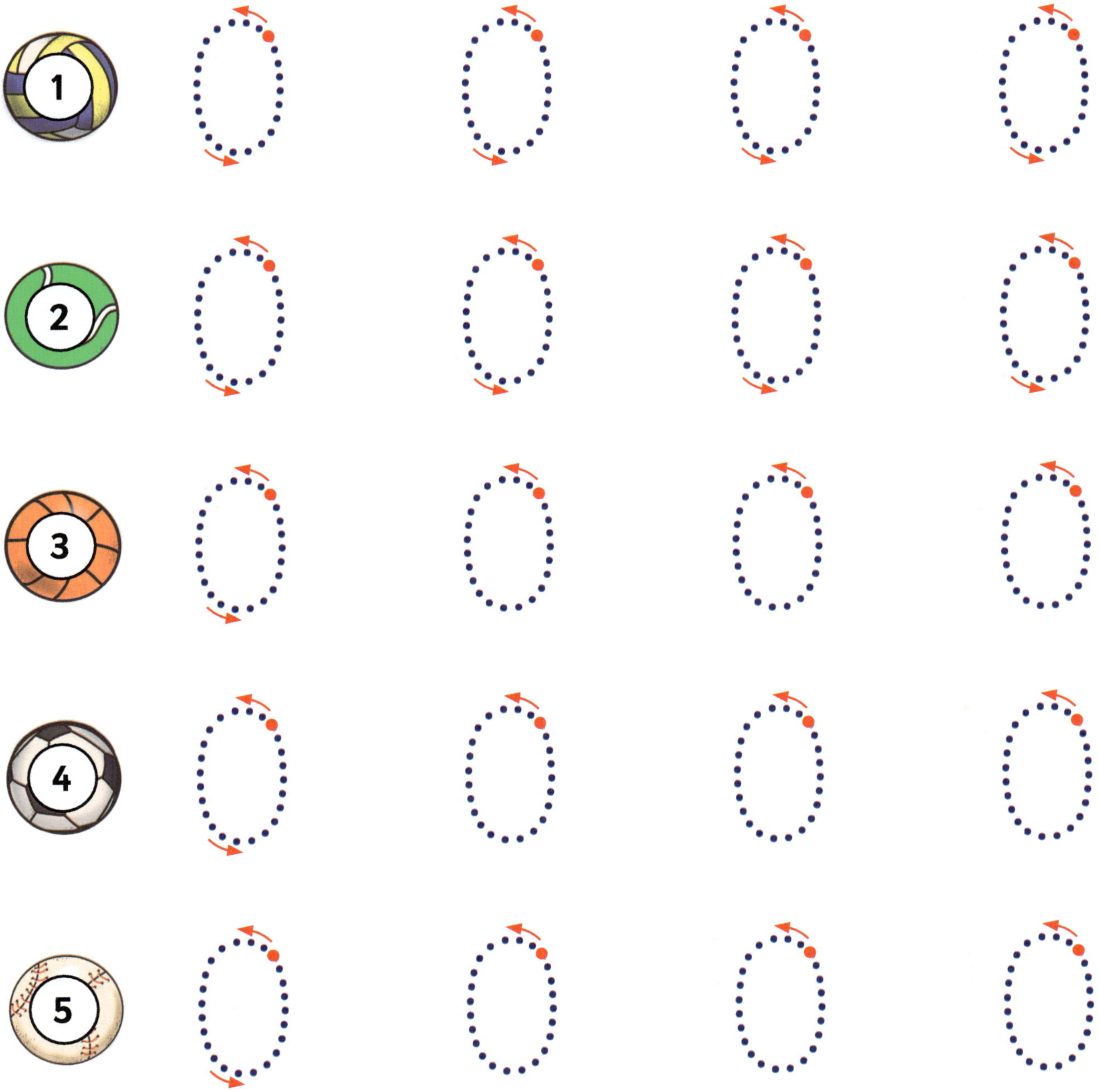

1. 0 0 0 0
2. 0 0 0 0
3. 0 0 0 0
4. 0 0 0 0
5. 0 0 0 0

How did you get on with this page?

Week 7 — Day 2

Start with your pencil on the red dots and trace these numbers. Then colour in the pictures.

How did you find tracing these numbers?

Week 7 — Day 3

Start at the red dots and trace these numbers.
Remember to follow the arrows.

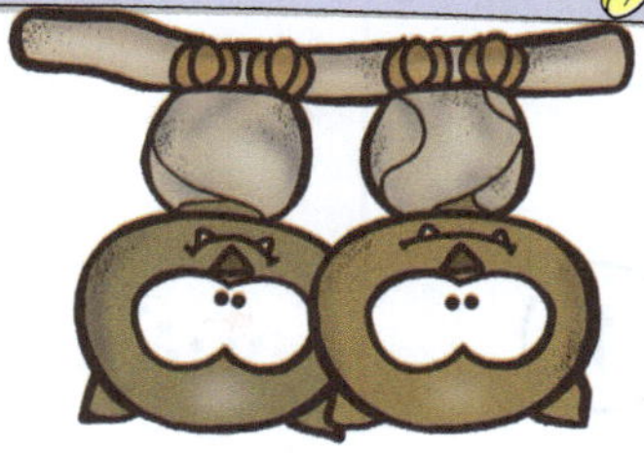

1. 2 2 2

2. 2 2 2 2

3. 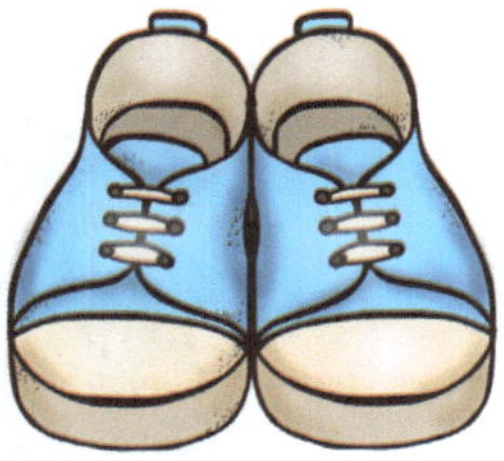 2 2 2

4. 2 2 2 2

5. 2 2 2

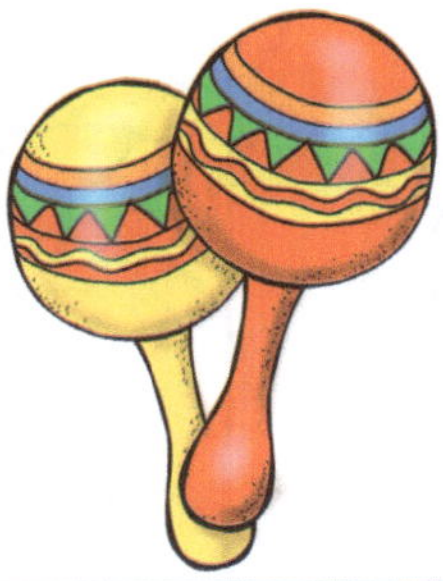

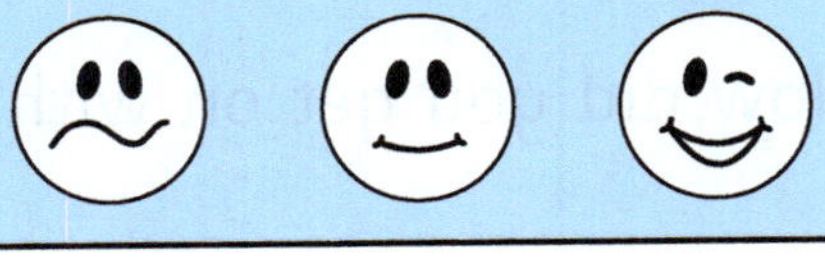

How well did you trace these numbers?

Week 7 — Day 5

Colour the picture using the numbers to help you.
Stripes has a sign showing the colour to use for each number.

How well do you think you did today?

Week 8 — Day 1

Start with your pencil on the red dots and trace these letters. Then colour in the unicorn.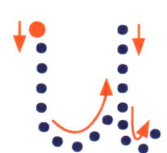

1)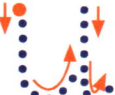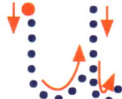

2)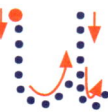

3)

4)

5)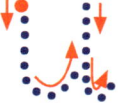

How did you get on with these letters?

Week 8 — Day 2

Trace these letters. Start at the red dots and use the arrows to help you.

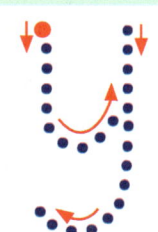 

1)

2)

3)

4)

5)

How did you find these letters?

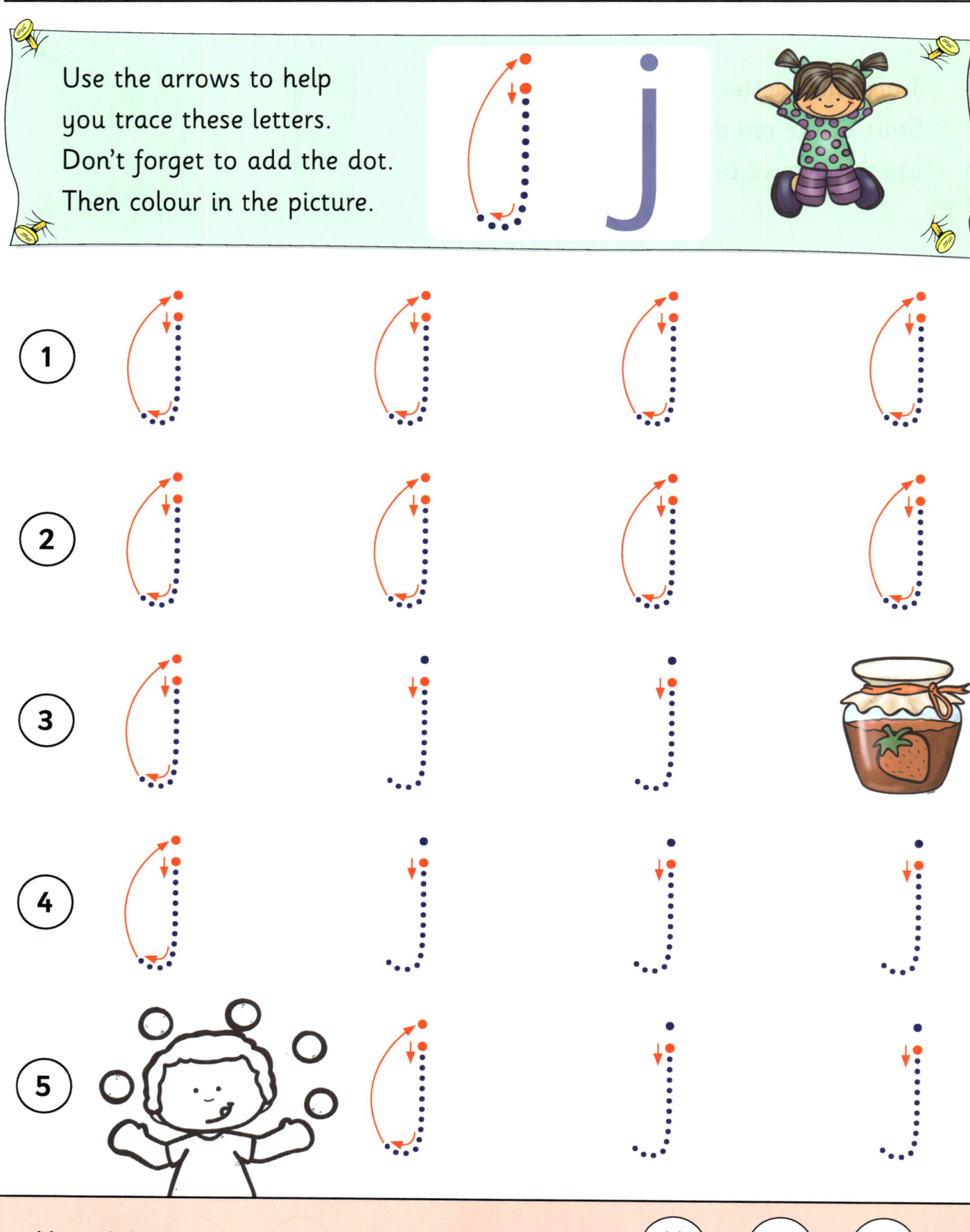

Week 8 — Day 5

Trace over the blue lines to show the path each person takes to their beach house. Then colour in Stripes' beach house.

How did you find this page?

Week 9 — Day 1

Trace these numbers.
You'll have to lift your pencil off the page for the second line that goes down.

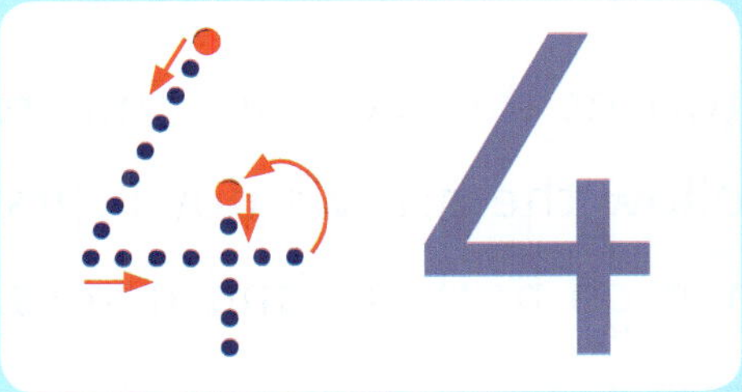

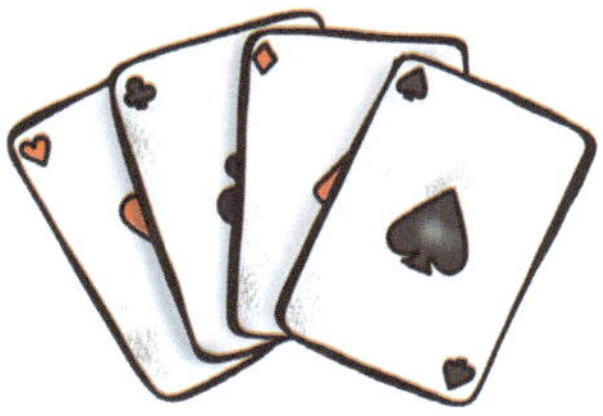

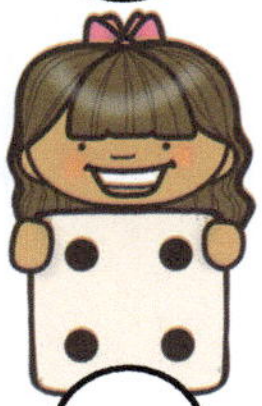

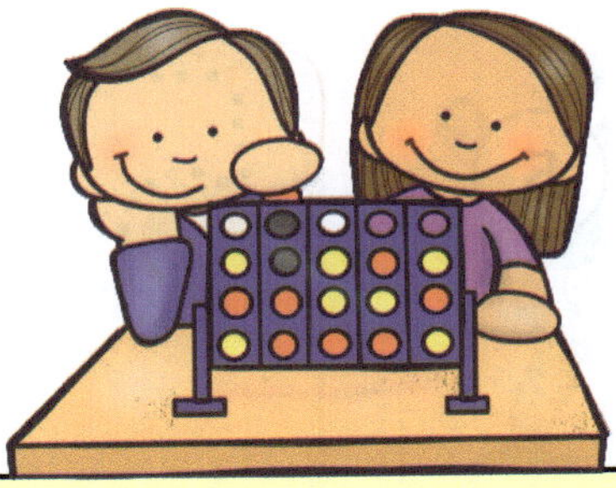

How did you get on with these numbers?

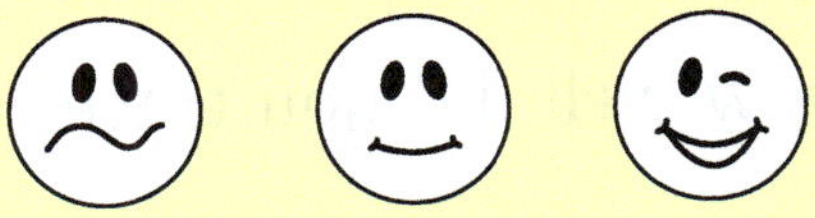

Week 9 — Day 2

Start at the red dots and trace these numbers. Follow the arrows down first, then go back up and across.

1.

2.

3.

4.

5.

How well did you trace these numbers?

Week 9 — Day 3

Start with your pencil on the red dots and trace these numbers. Then colour in the cake.

How did you get on with this page?

Week 9 — Day 4

Trace over the lines to complete the numbers. Then colour in the drum.

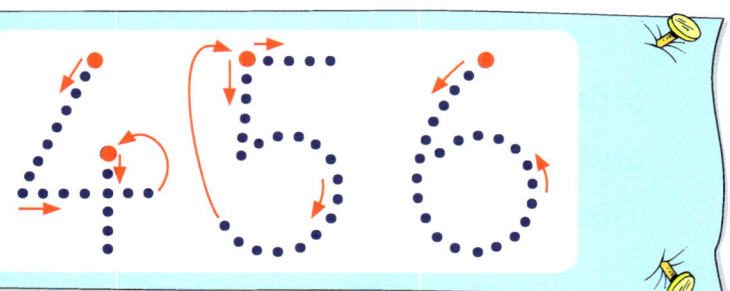

1. 4 4 4 4
2. 5 5 5 5
3. 6 6 6
4. 0 1 2 3
5. 4 5 6

How did you do with these numbers?

Reception Handwriting — Autumn Term

Week 9 — Day 5

Stripes has lots of birthday presents. Draw lines to match each group of presents to the right number. Then colour in the numbers.

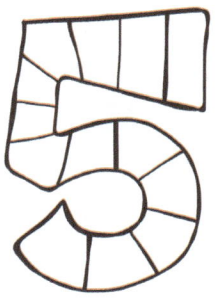

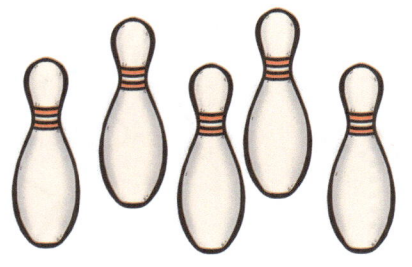

How well do you think you did today?

Week 10 — Day 1

Start at the red dots and trace these letters.
Follow the arrows down, then back up and round.
When you've finished, colour in the rabbits.

1. 
2.
3. 
4.
5.

How did you find these letters?

Week 10 — Day 2

Follow the arrows to trace these letters. When you've finished, colour in the ninjas.

How did you get on with these letters?

Week 10 — Day 3

Start with your pencil on the red dots and trace these letters. Use the arrows to help you.

m m

1 m m m m

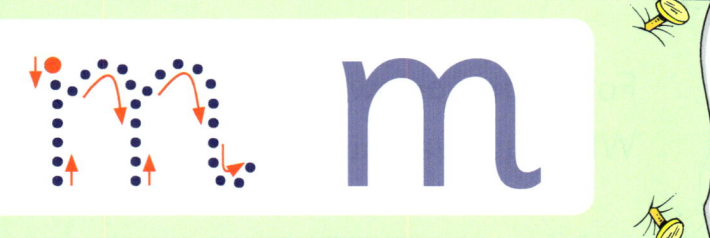

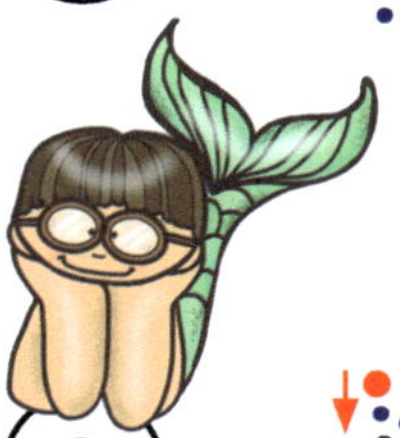

2 m m m m

3 m m m

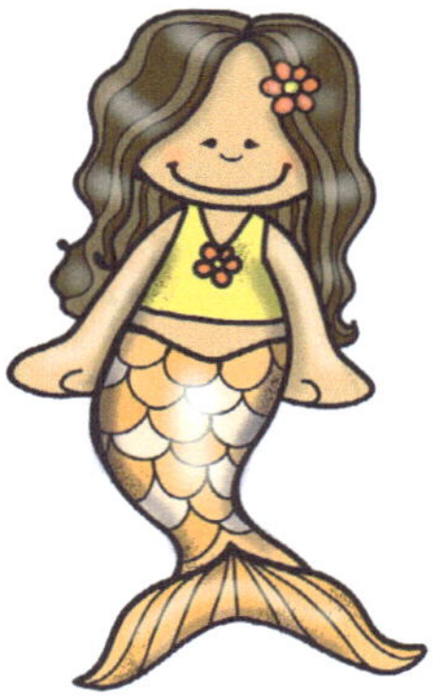

4 m m m m

5

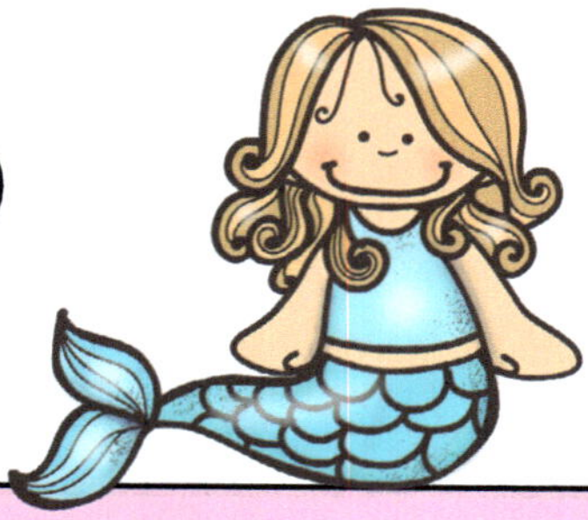

m m m

How did you get on with this page?

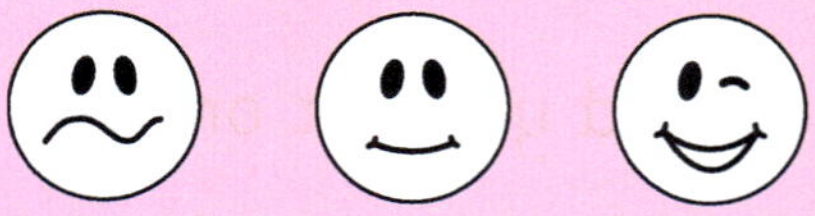

Week 10 — Day 5

Draw a line along the path to help Stripes get to the planet.
Try to stay in the middle of the path.
When you've finished, colour in the rocket ship.

How did you find this page?

Week 11 — Day 1

Follow the arrows to trace these numbers.
Start with your pencil on the red dot.

1.

2.

3.

4.

5.

How did you find these numbers?

Week 11 — Day 2

Start at the red dots and trace these numbers.
When you've finished, colour in the bats.

1.
2.
3.
4.
5.

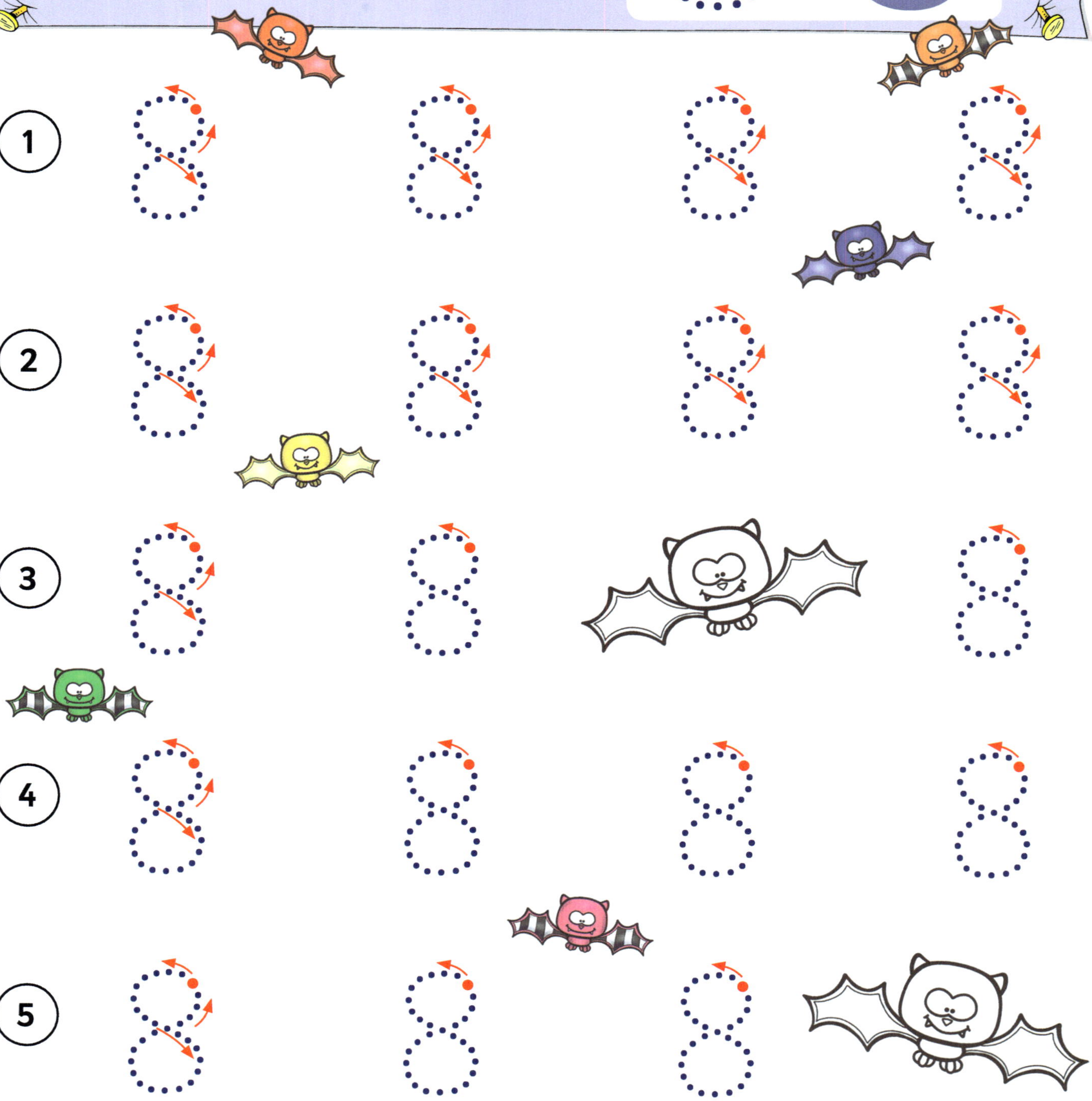

How did you get on with these numbers?

Week 11 — Day 3

Start with your pencil on the red dots and trace these numbers. Then colour in the pictures.

1.
2.
3.
4.
5.

How well did you trace these numbers?

Week 11 — Day 4

Trace over the lines to complete the numbers.
Remember to start with your pencil on the red dots.
Then circle the bigger number in each cloud.

1) 1, 0   7, 2
2) 3, 6   4, 0
3) 5, 2   9, 1
4) 8, 6   4, 5
5) 3, 8   7, 9

How did you get on with this page?

Week 11 — Day 5

Stripes is at a Christmas party. Trace over the dashed lines to draw patterns on the crackers. Then colour them in.

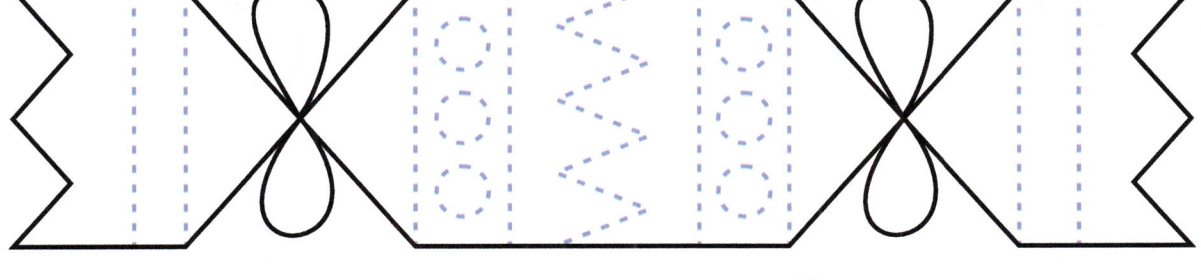

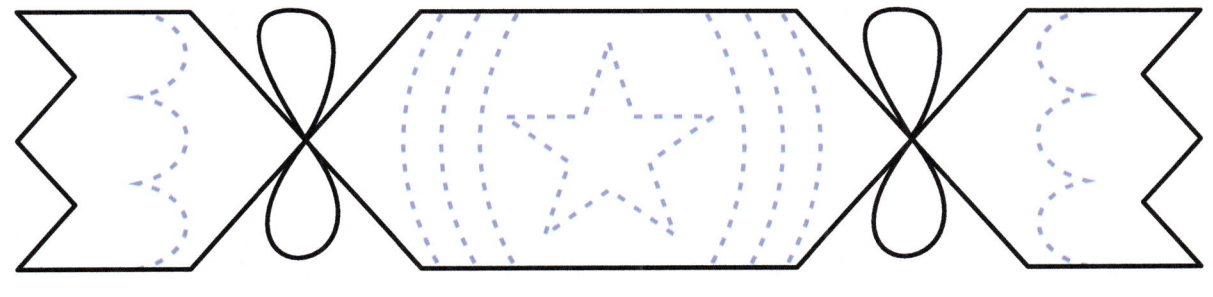

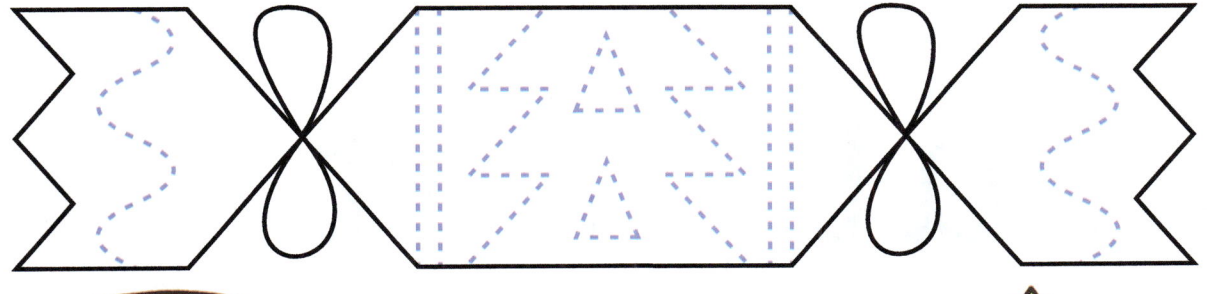

How did you get on with these pictures?

Week 12 — Day 1

Trace these letters. Start at the red dots and follow the arrows. Then colour in the picture.

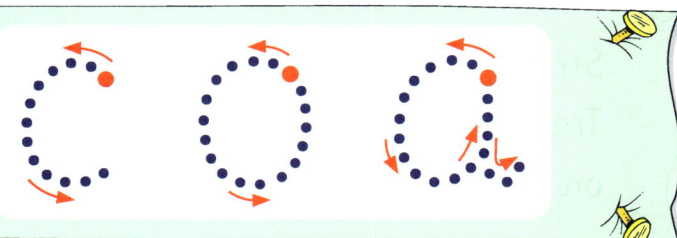

1)

2)

3)

4)

5)

How did you get on with these letters?

Week 12 — Day 2

Start with your pencil on the red dots and trace these letters. Then colour in the picture.

1. i i i i i
2. l l l l l
3. t t t t t

4. pig log
5. toy

How did you find tracing these letters?

Week 12 — Day 3

Follow the arrows to trace these letters. When you've finished, colour in the jogger.

1. u u u u u

2. y y y y y

3. j j j j j

4. tug

5. yes jog

How did you find this page?

Week 12 — Day 4

Start at the red dots and trace these letters. Then colour in the picture.

r n m

1) r r r r r

2) n n n n n

3) m m m m m

4) red man

5) net

How well did you trace these letters?

Week 12 — Day 5

Stripes is visiting the North Pole. There are 6 differences between the pictures below. Draw a circle around each difference. When you've finished, colour in the reindeer and sleigh.

How did you get on with this page?